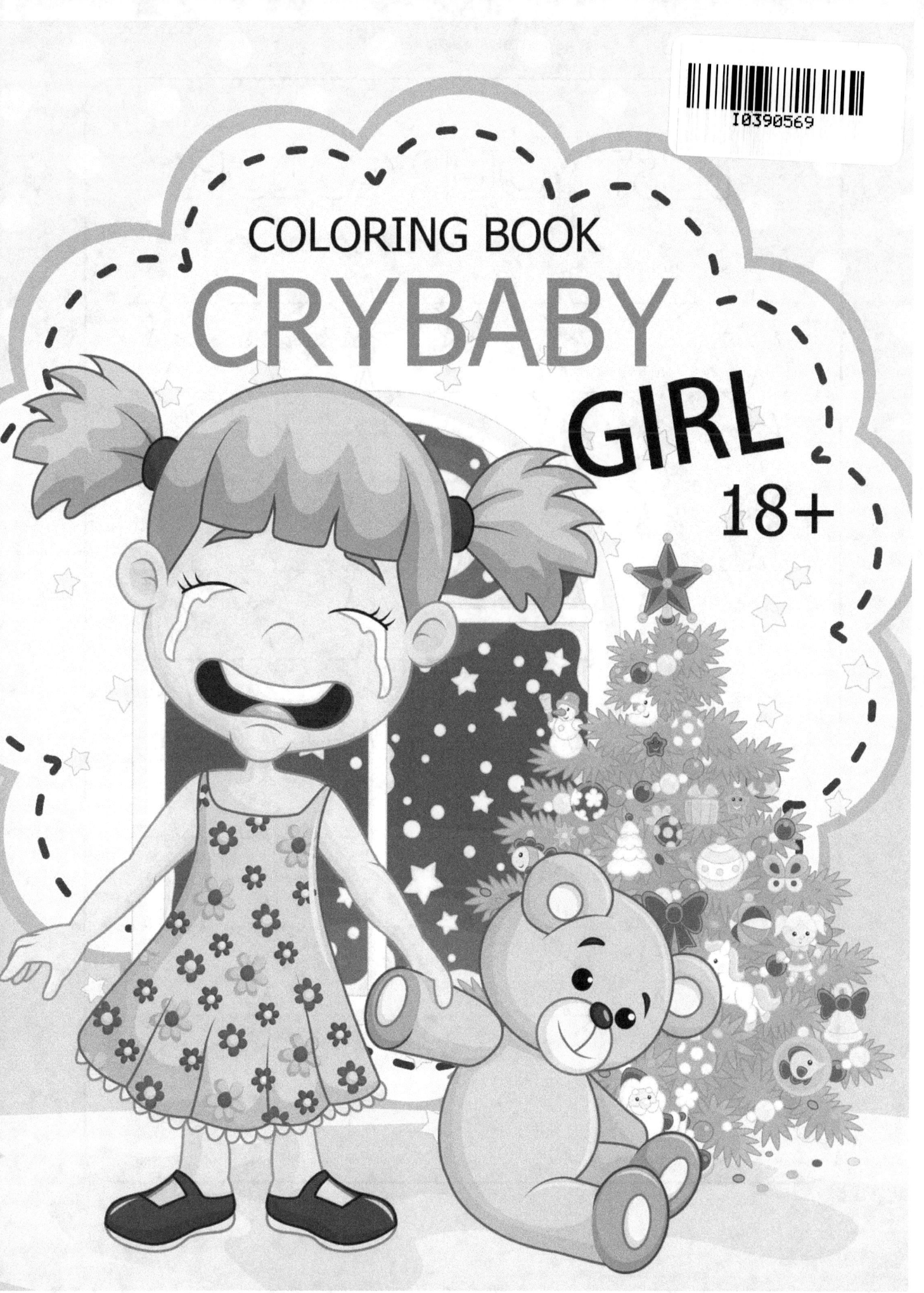

COLORING BOOK
CRYBABY
GIRL
18+

TEST YOUR COLOR

TEST YOUR COLOR

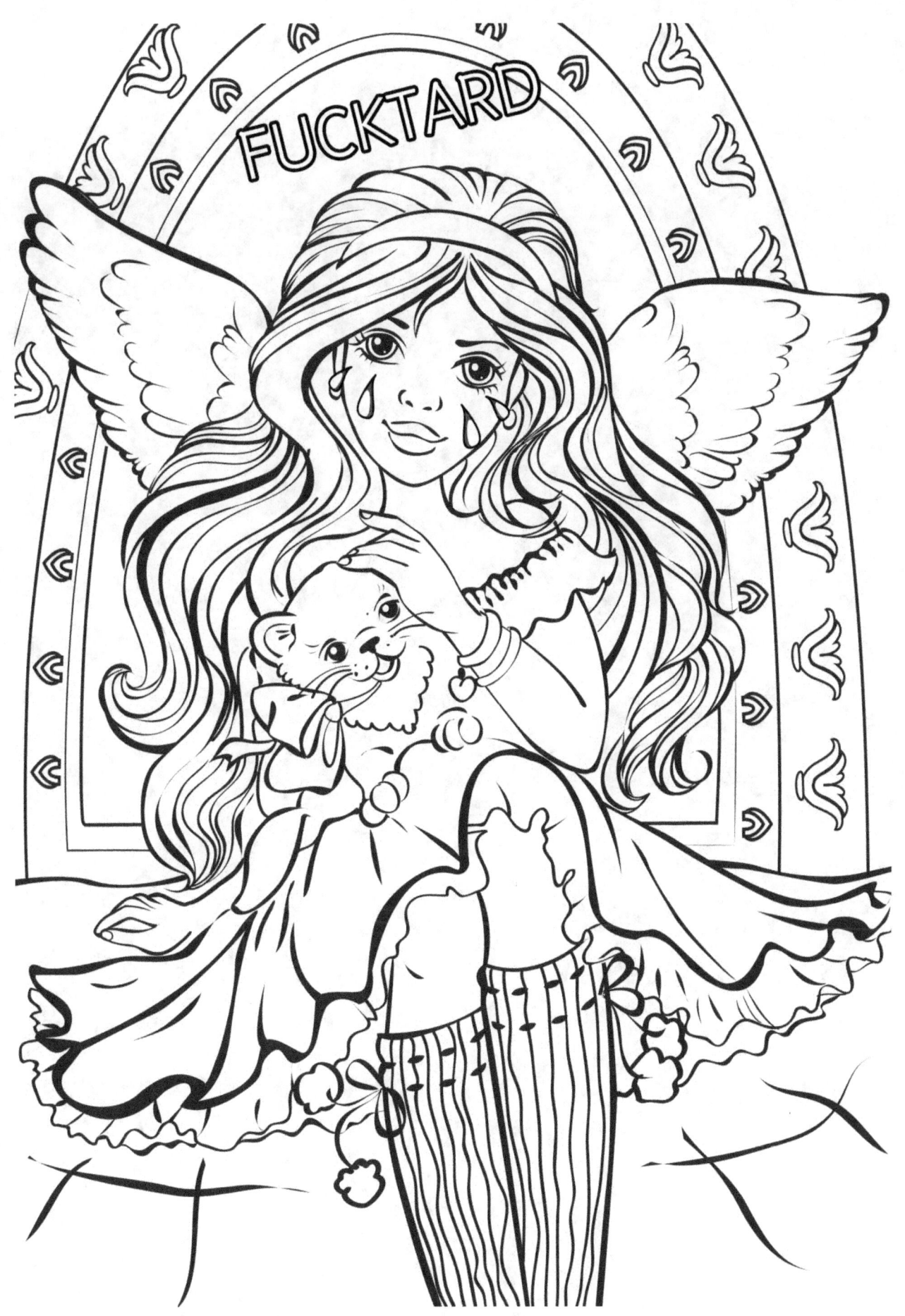

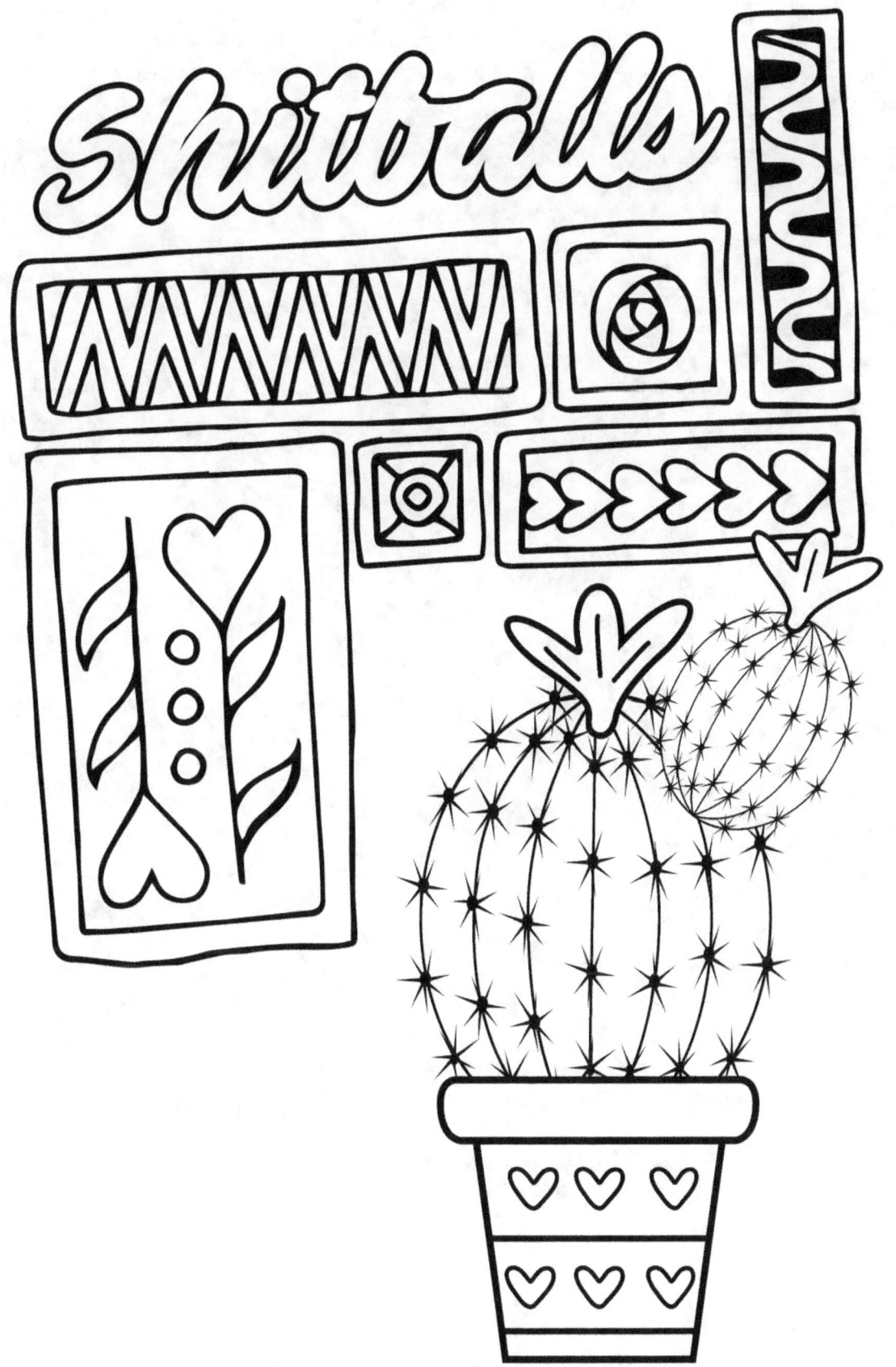

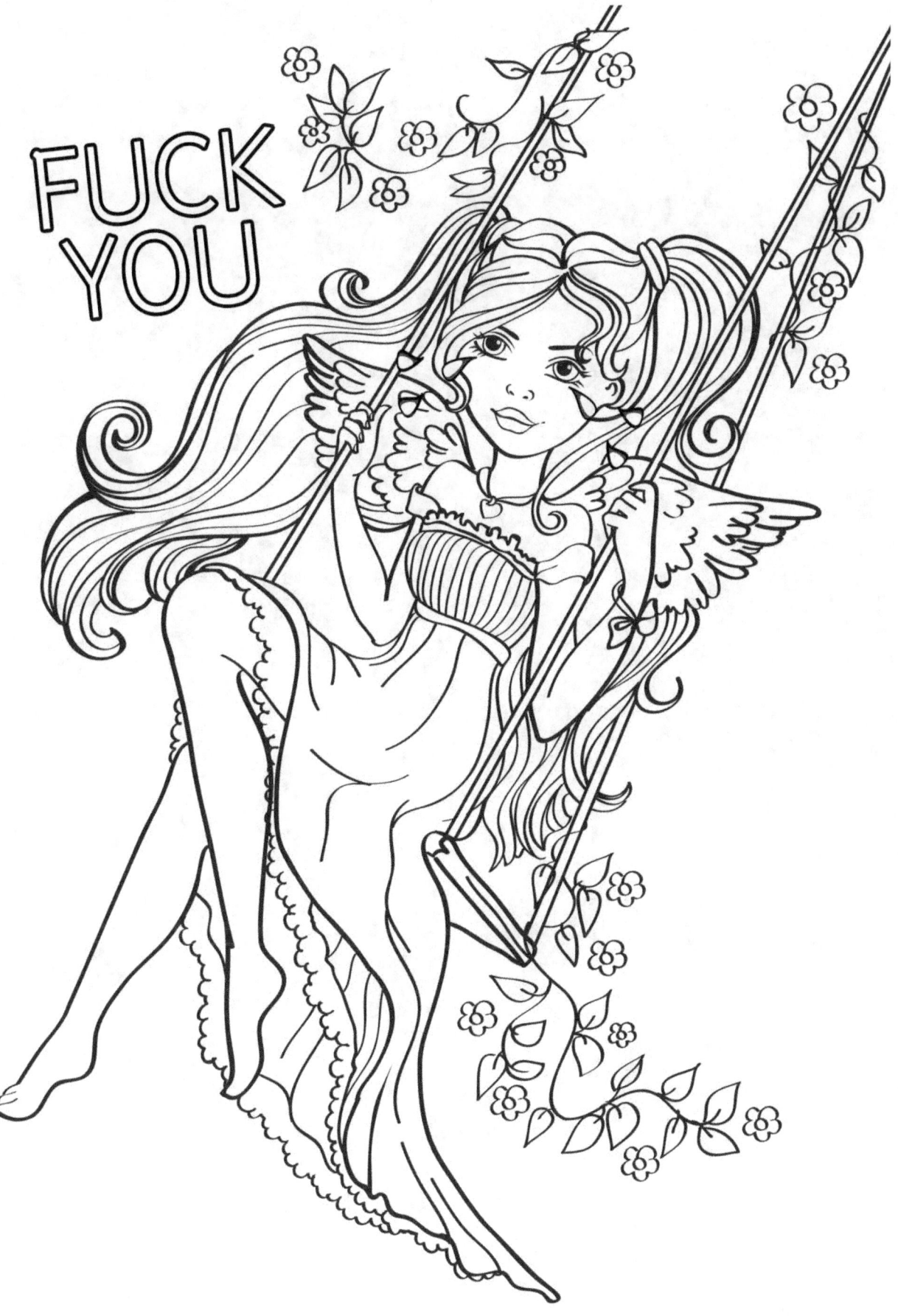

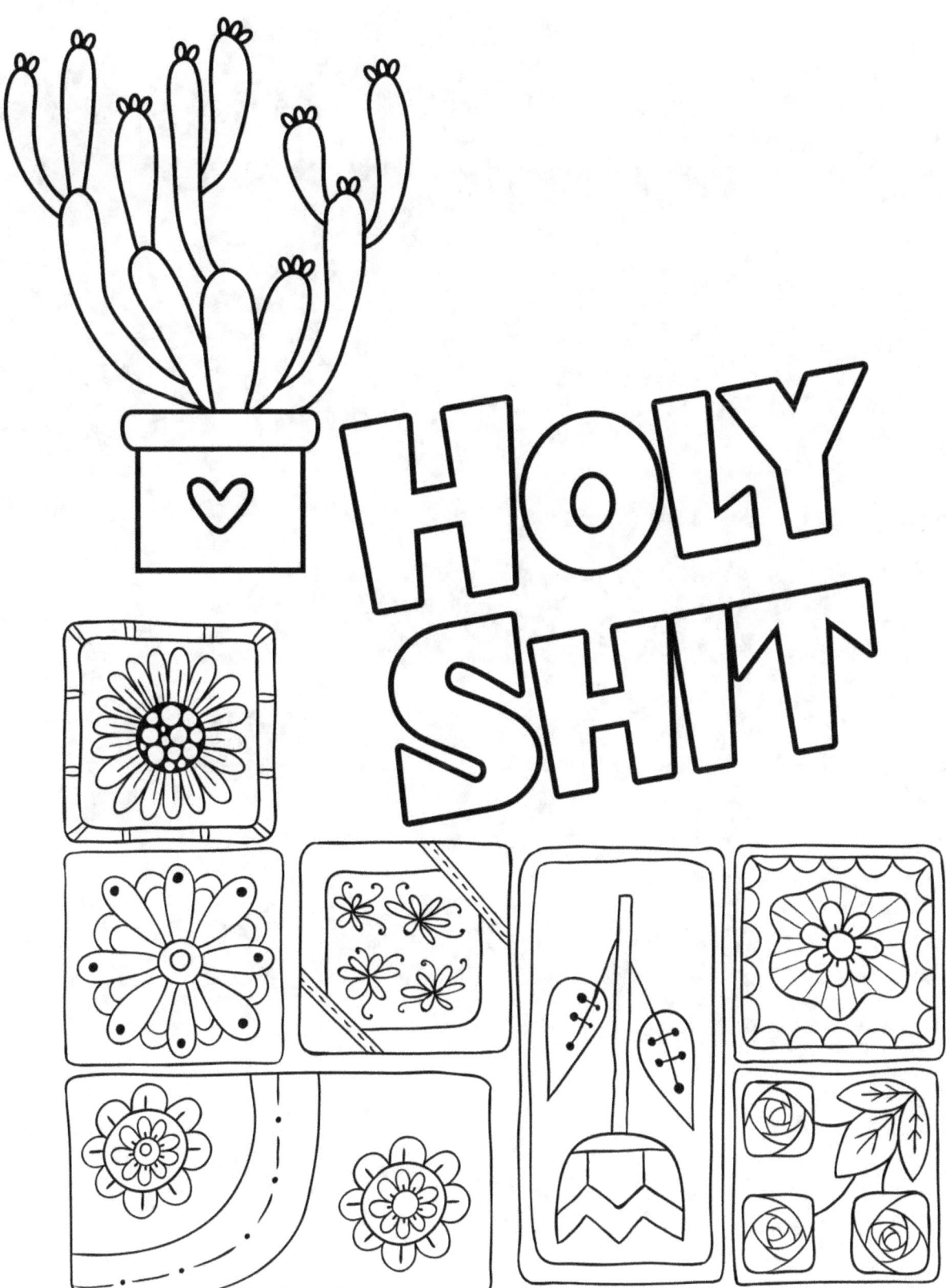

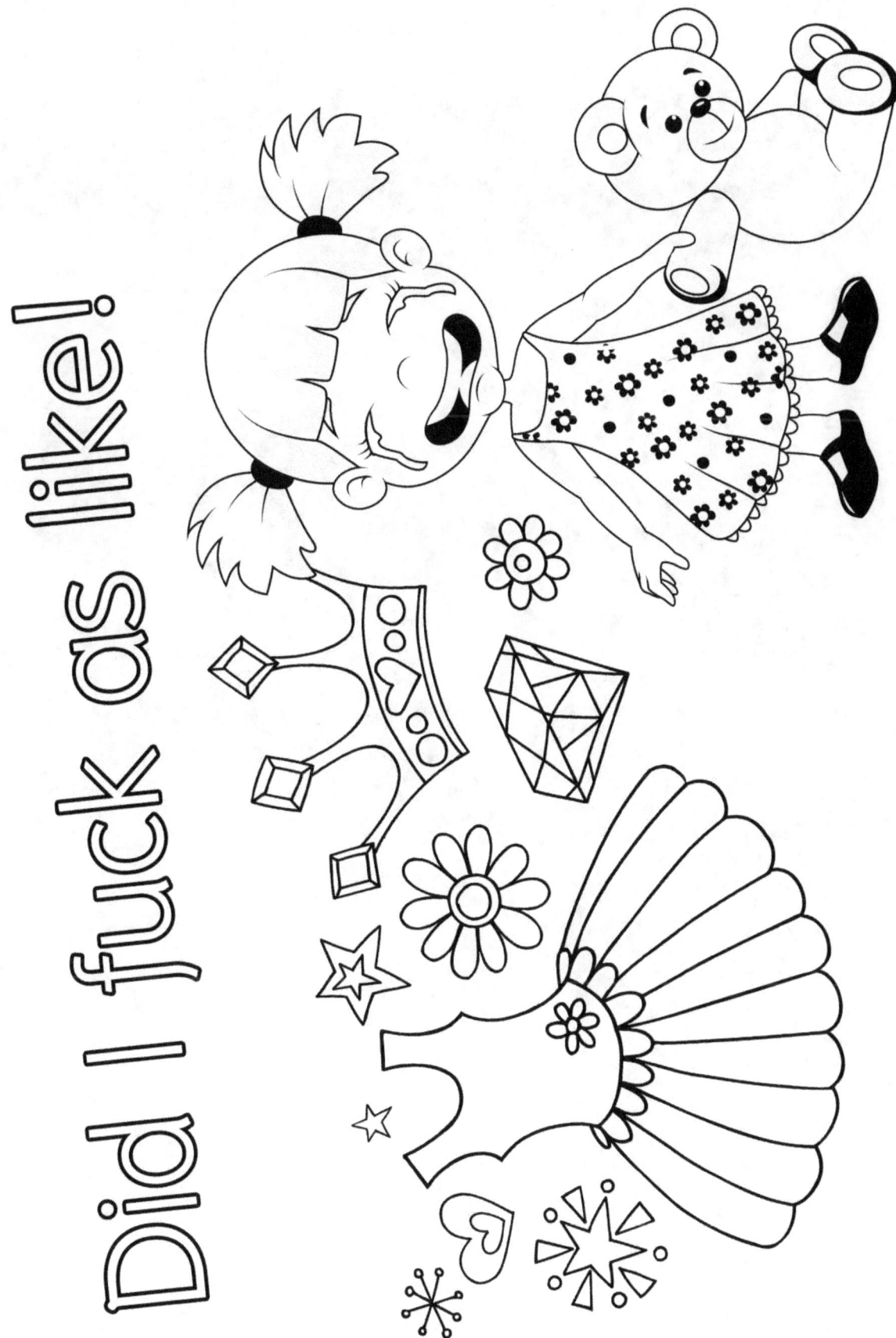

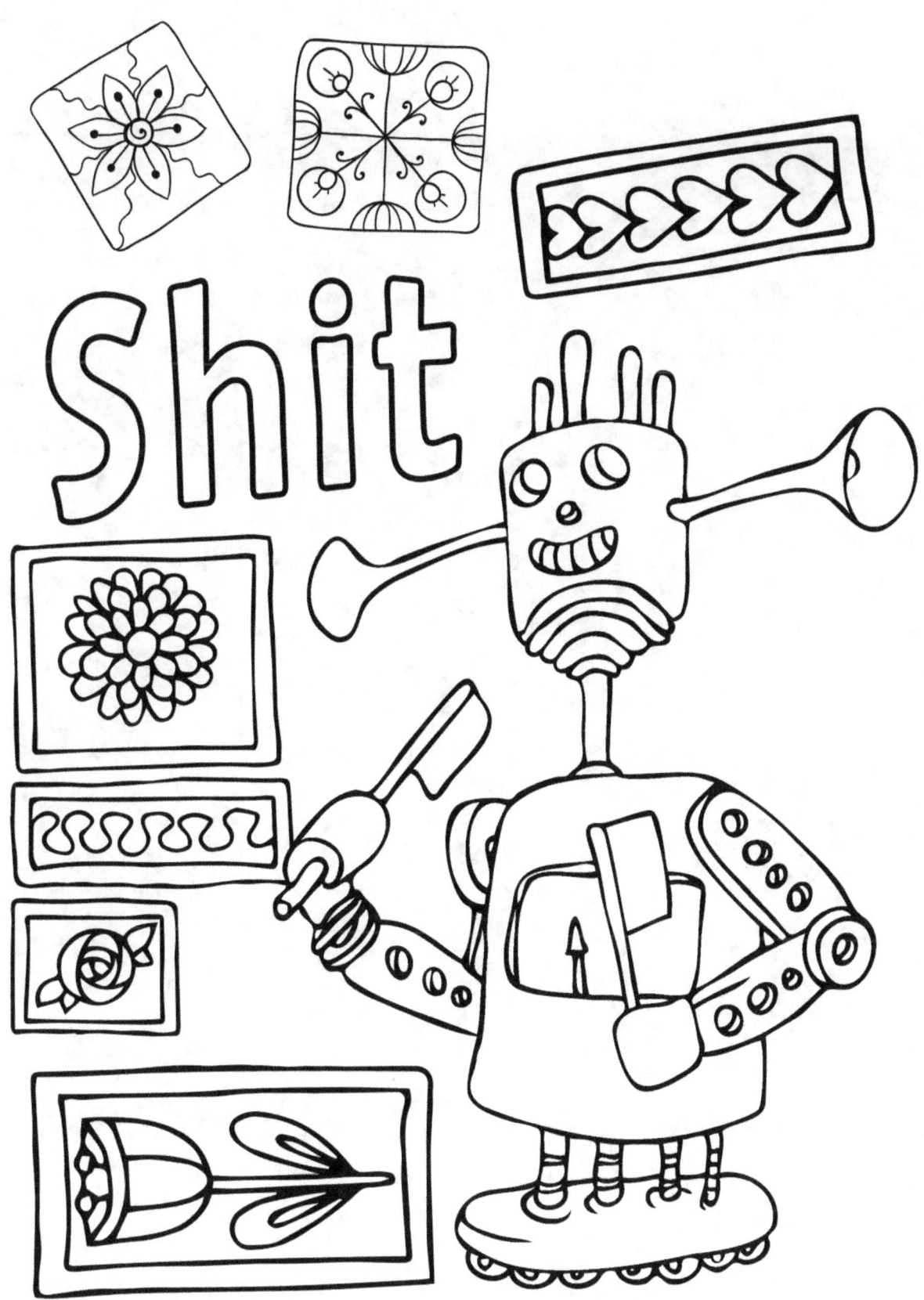

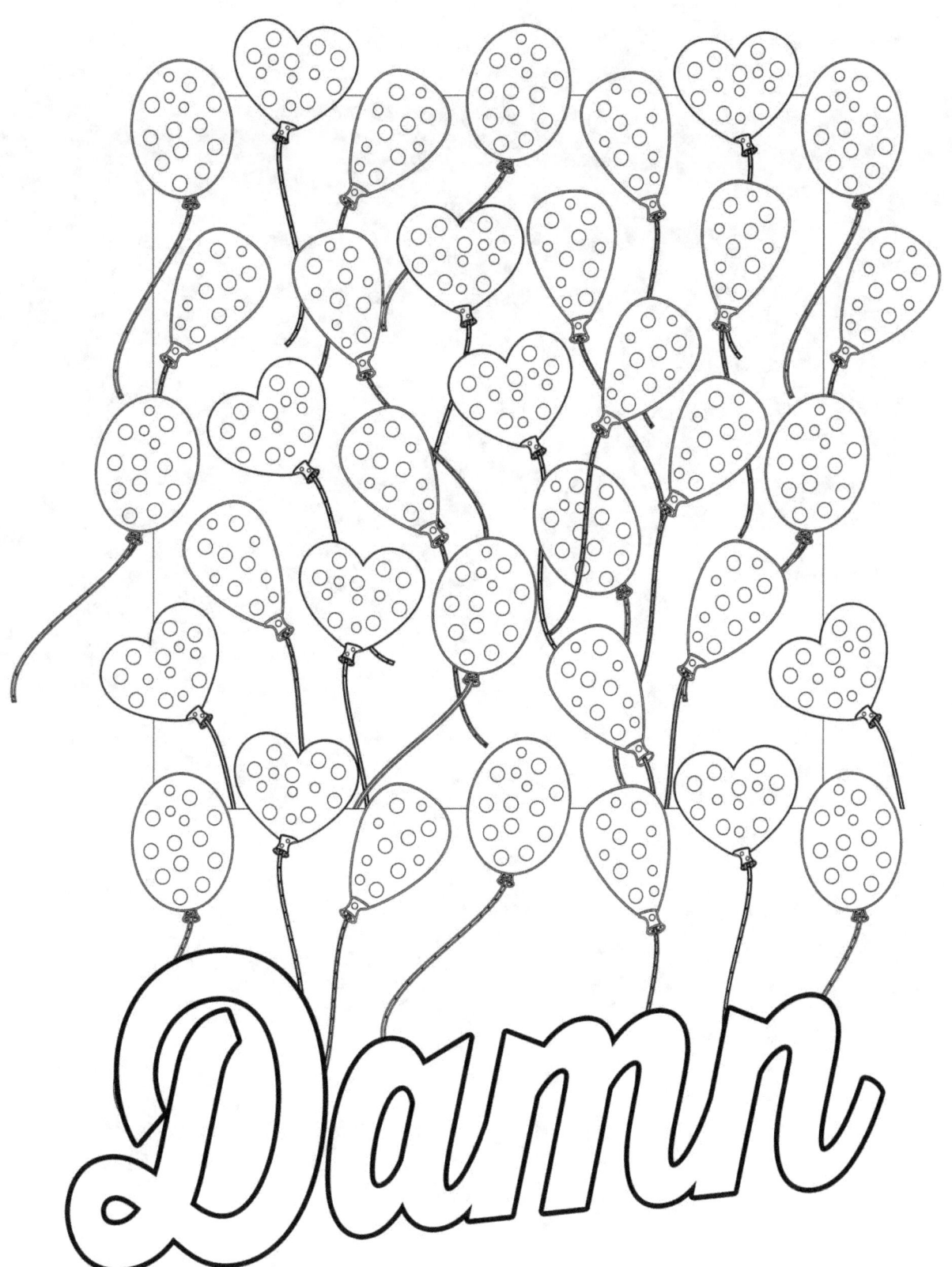

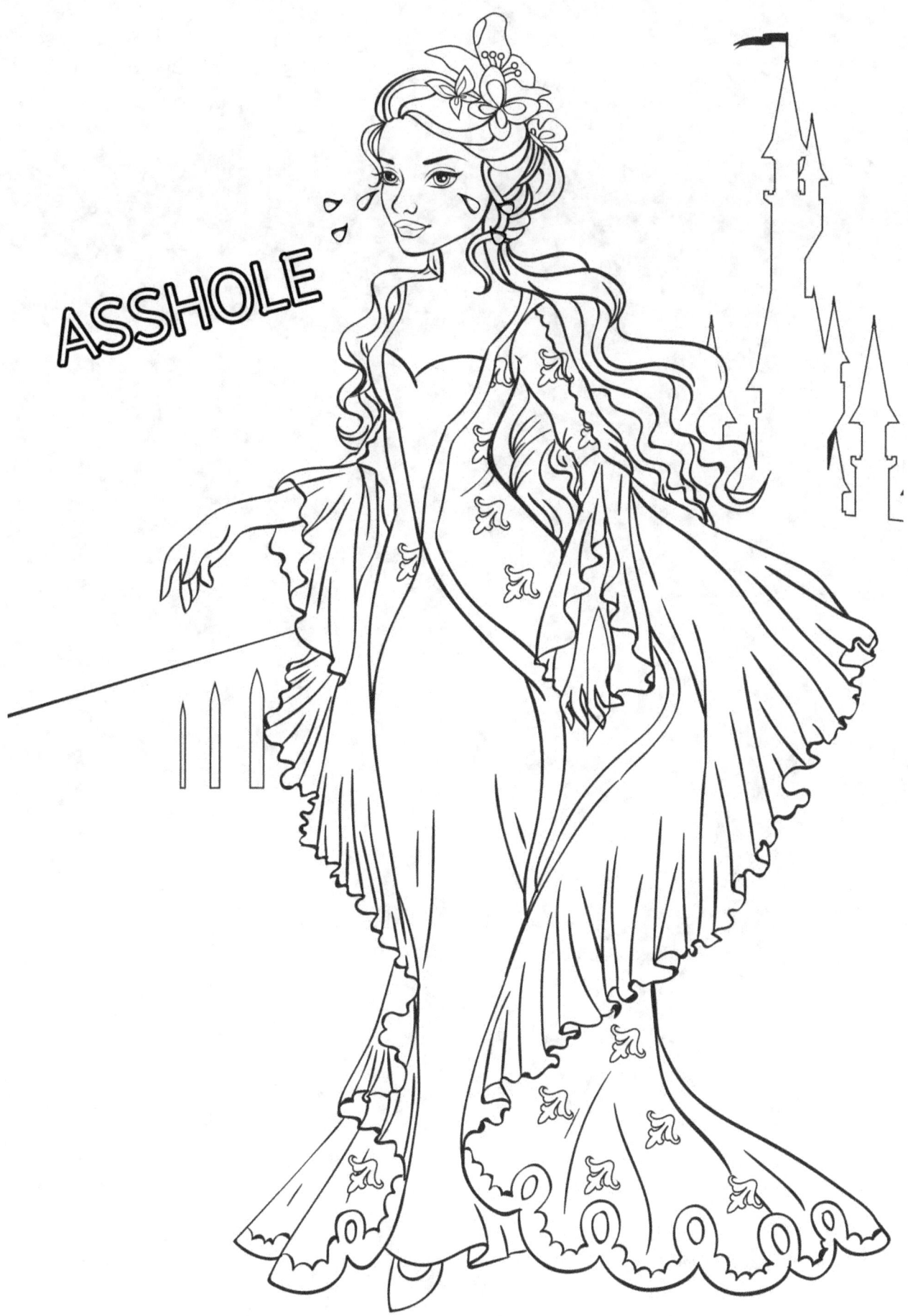

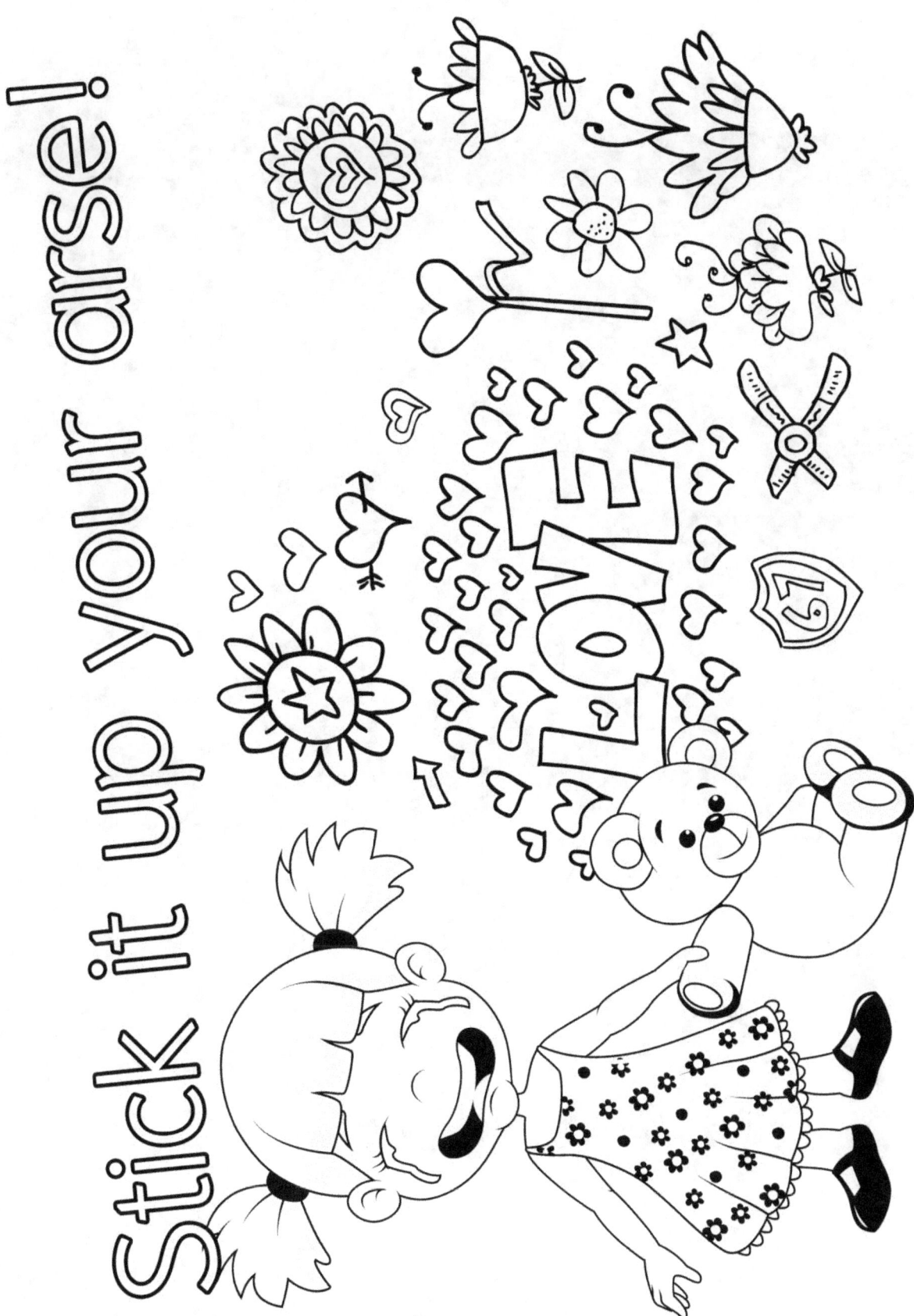

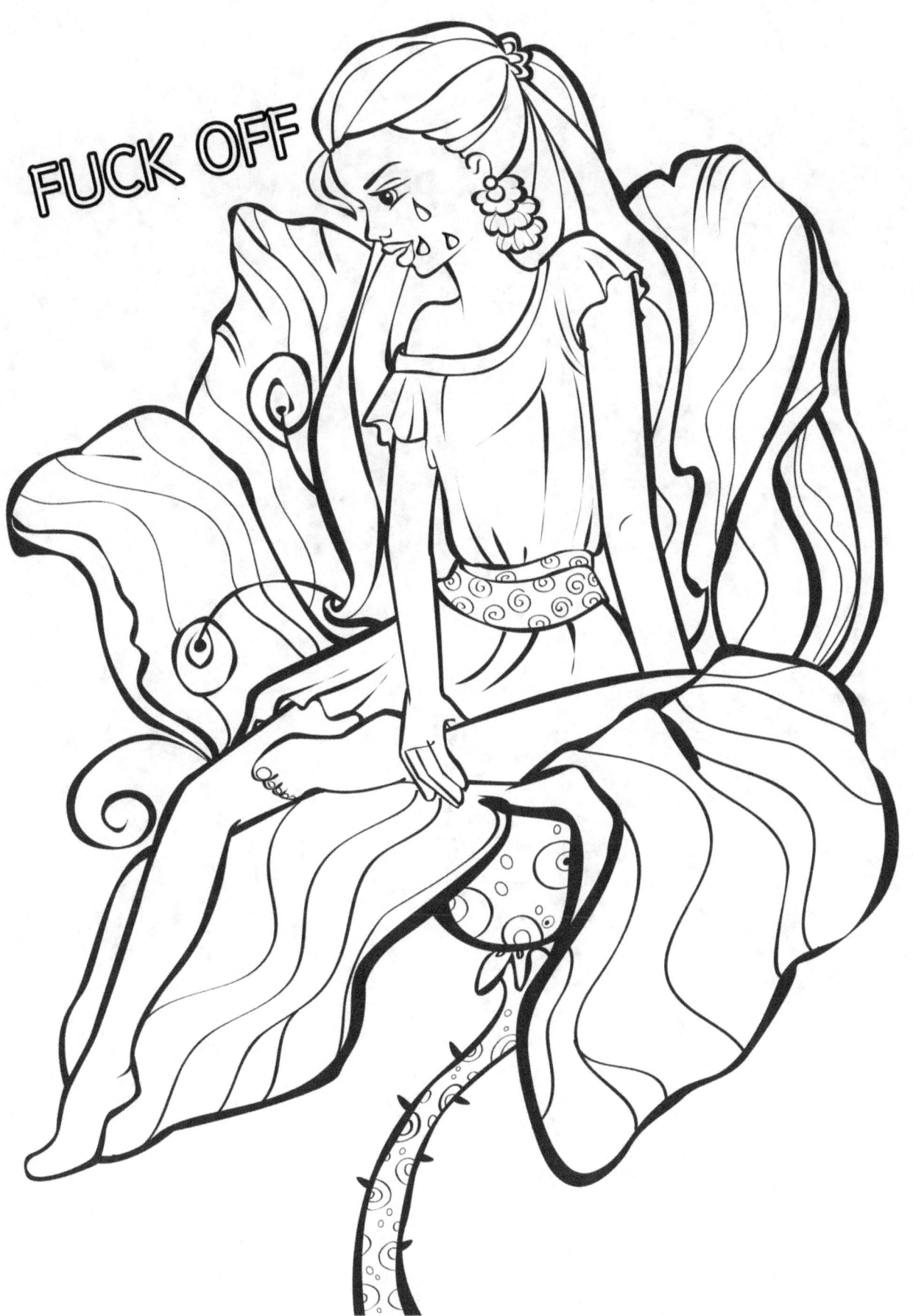

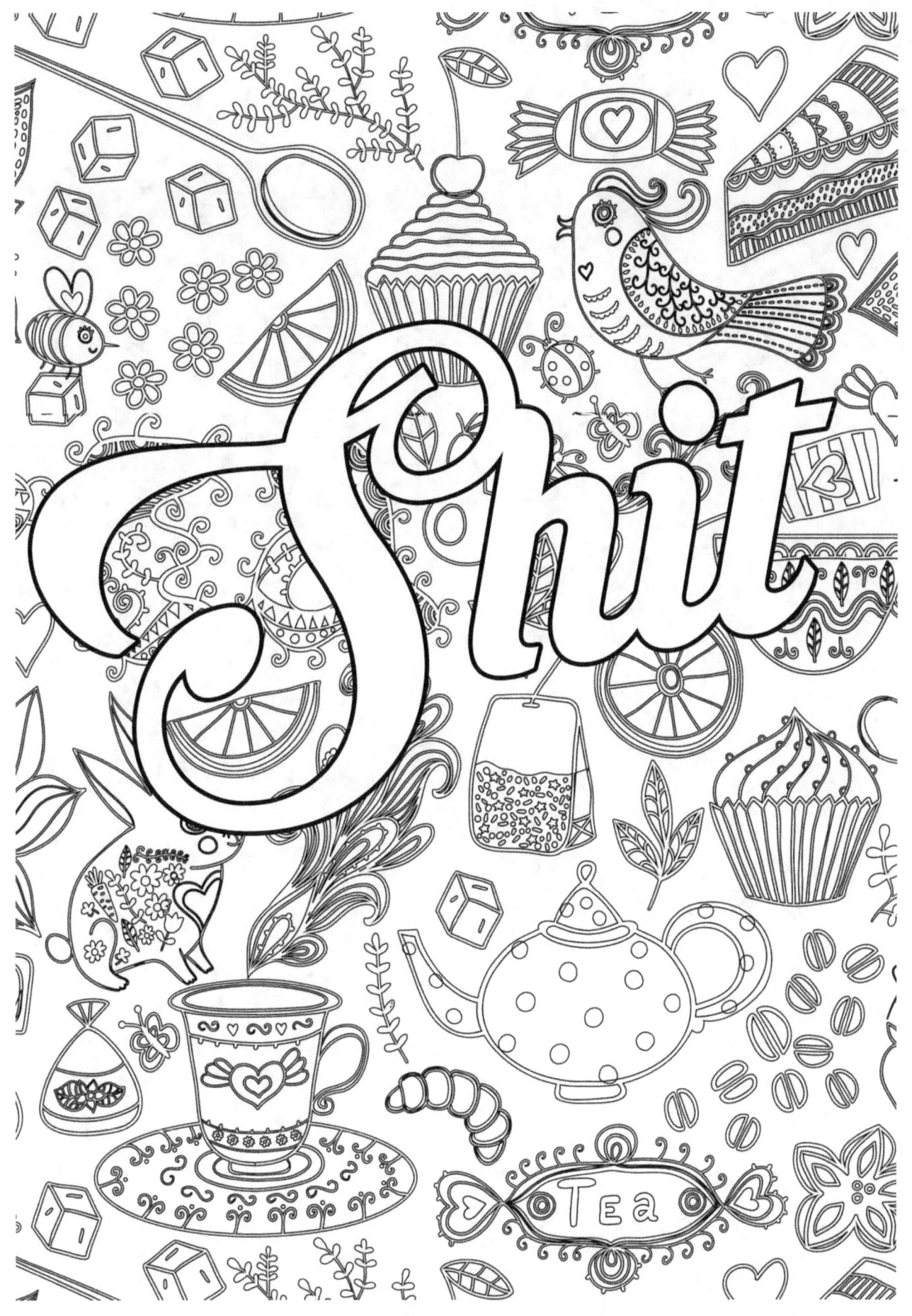

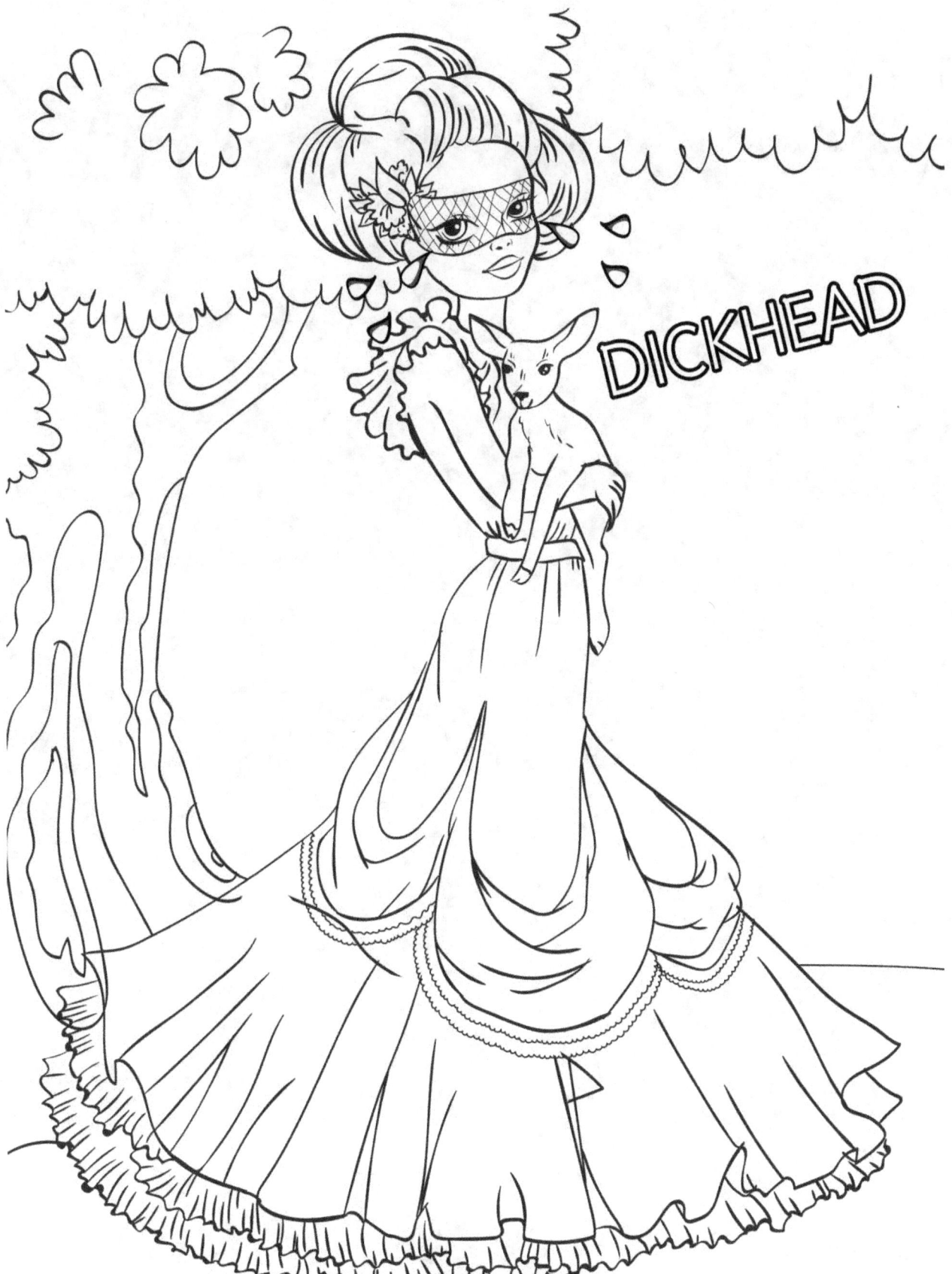

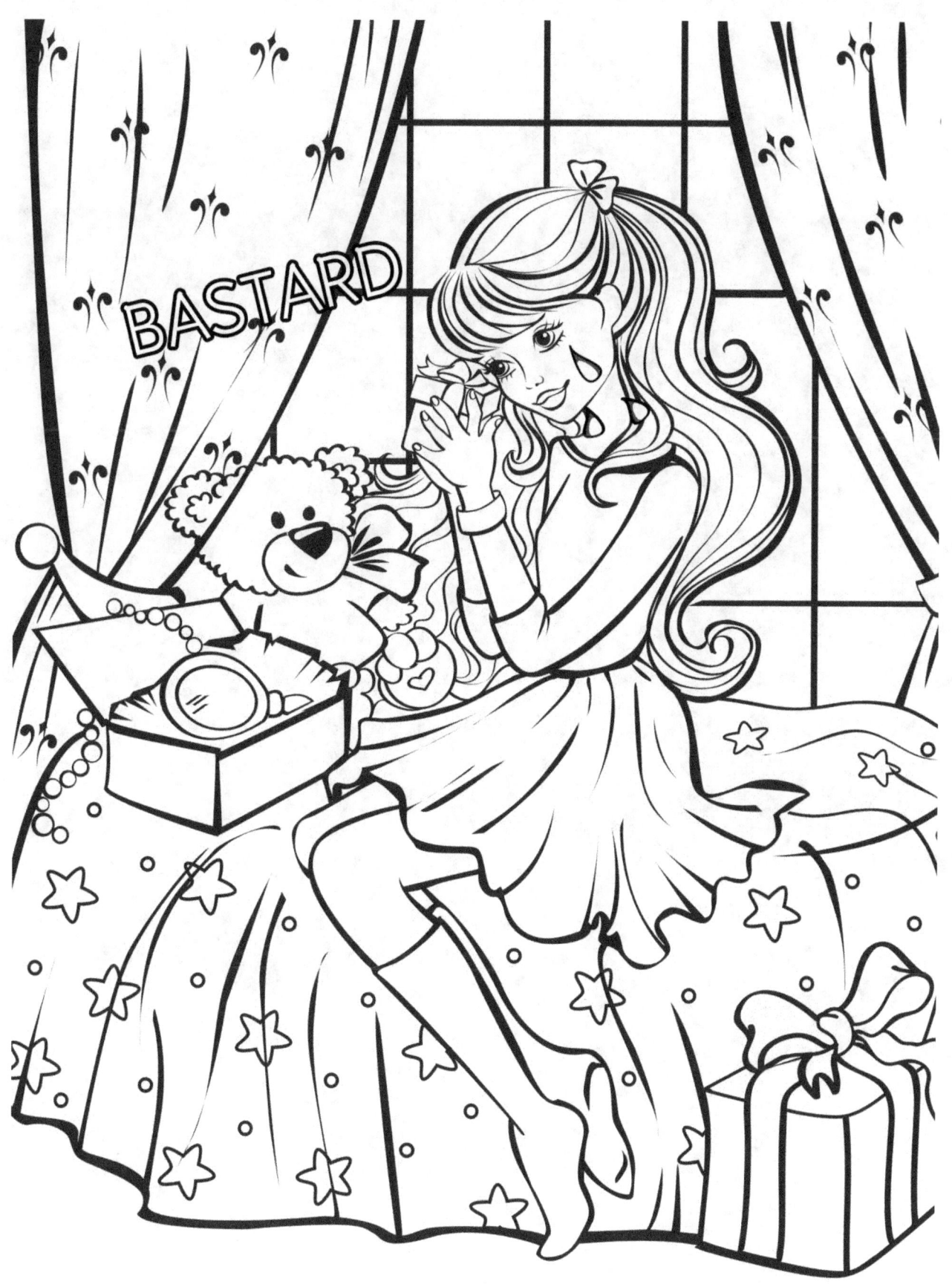

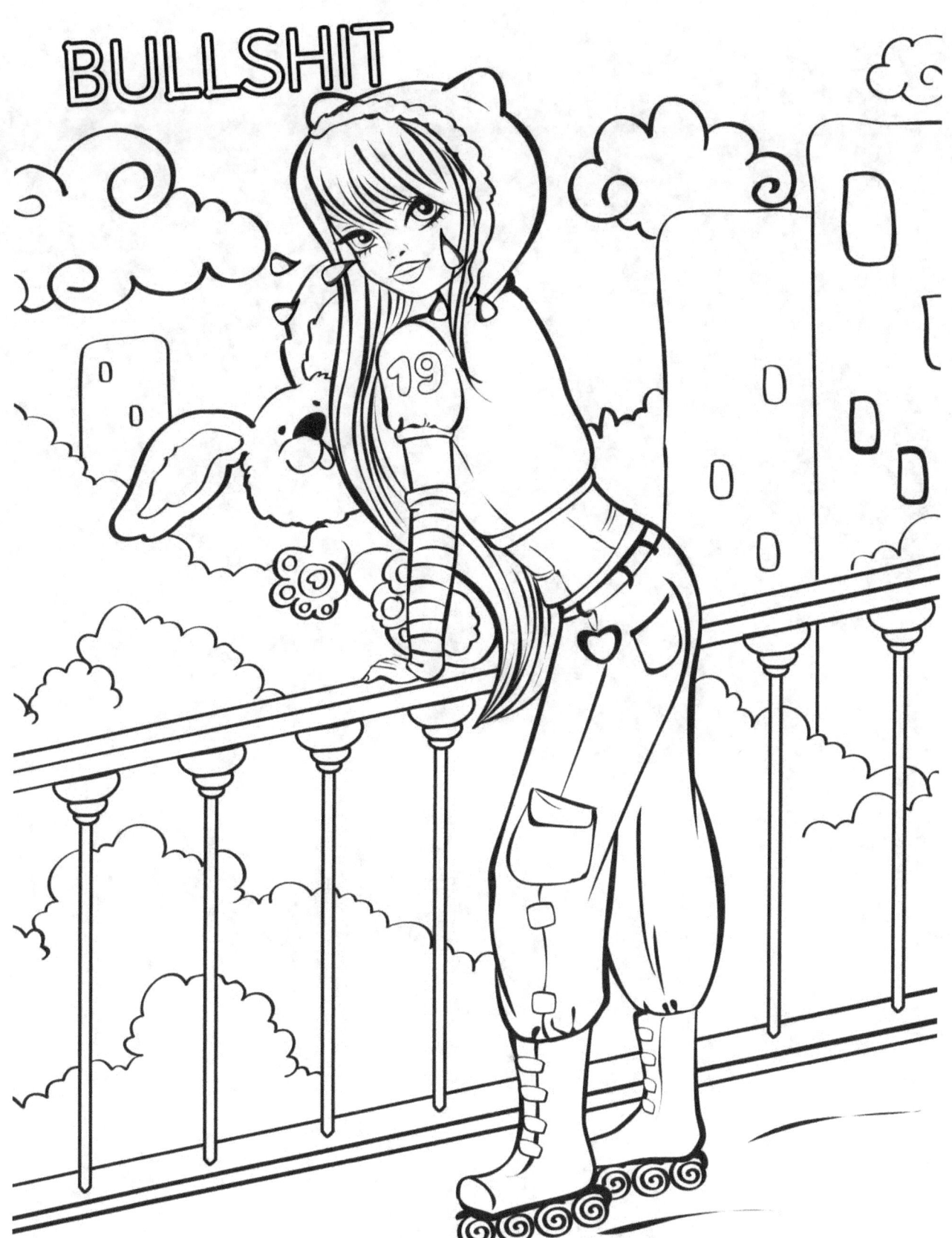

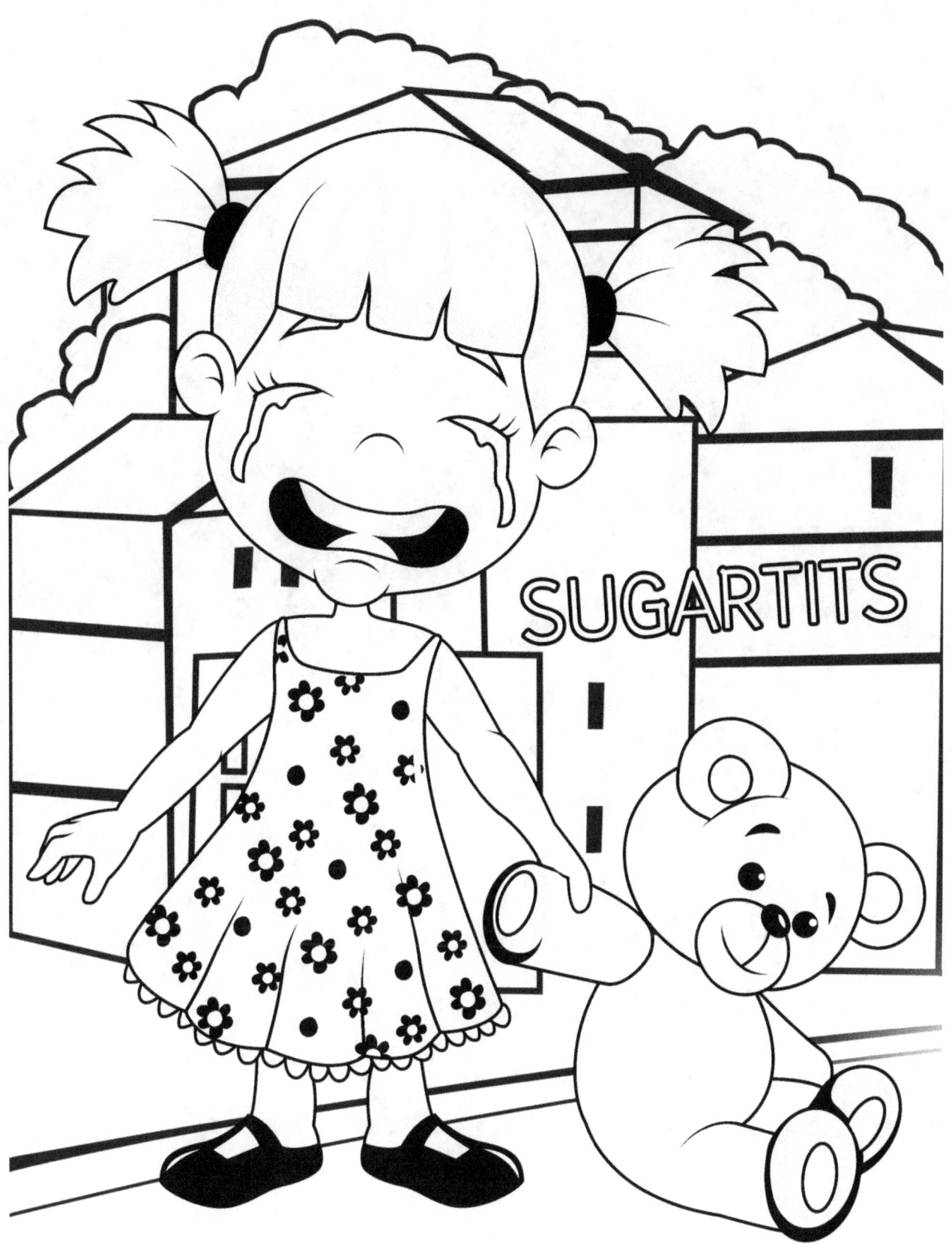

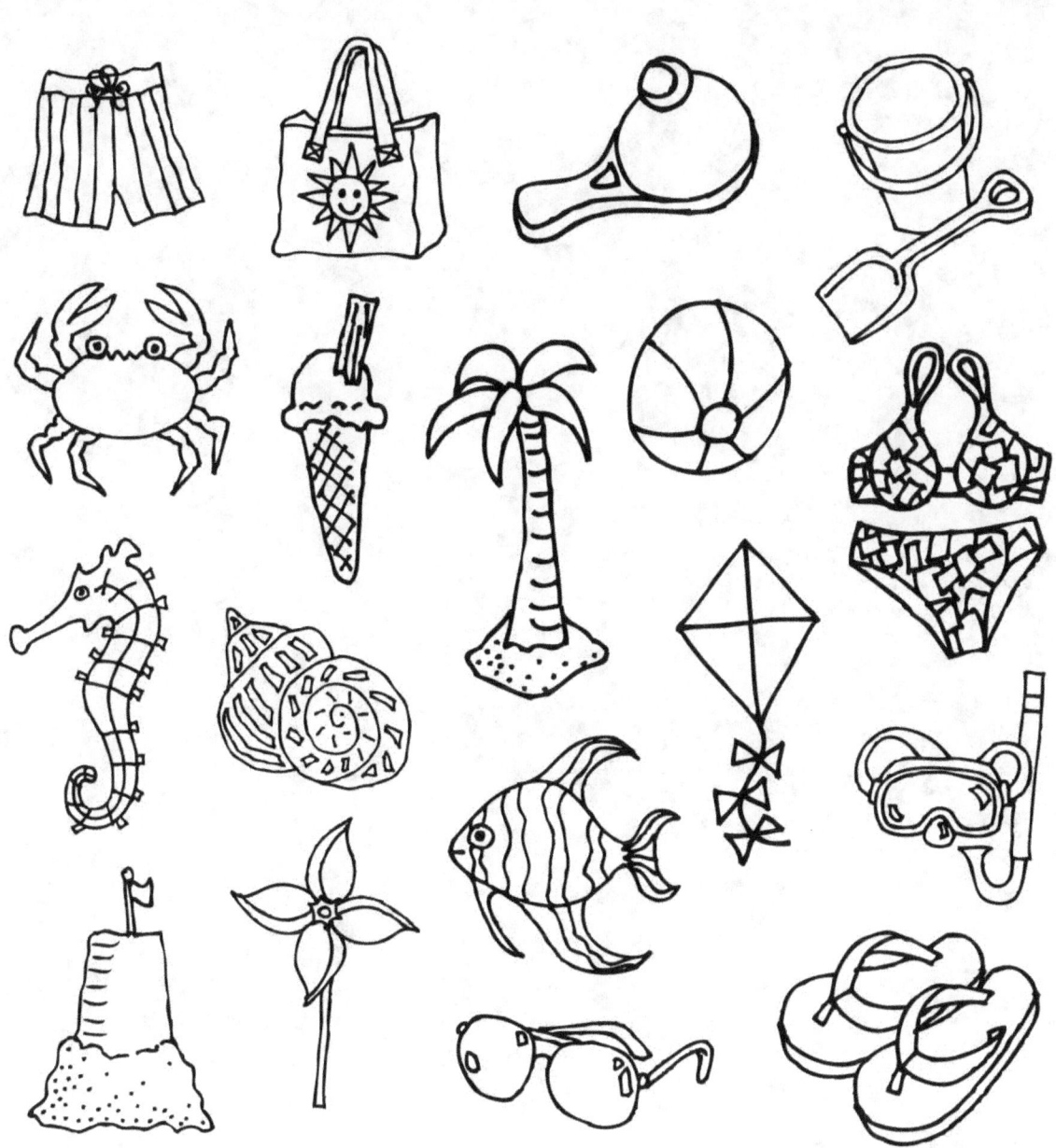

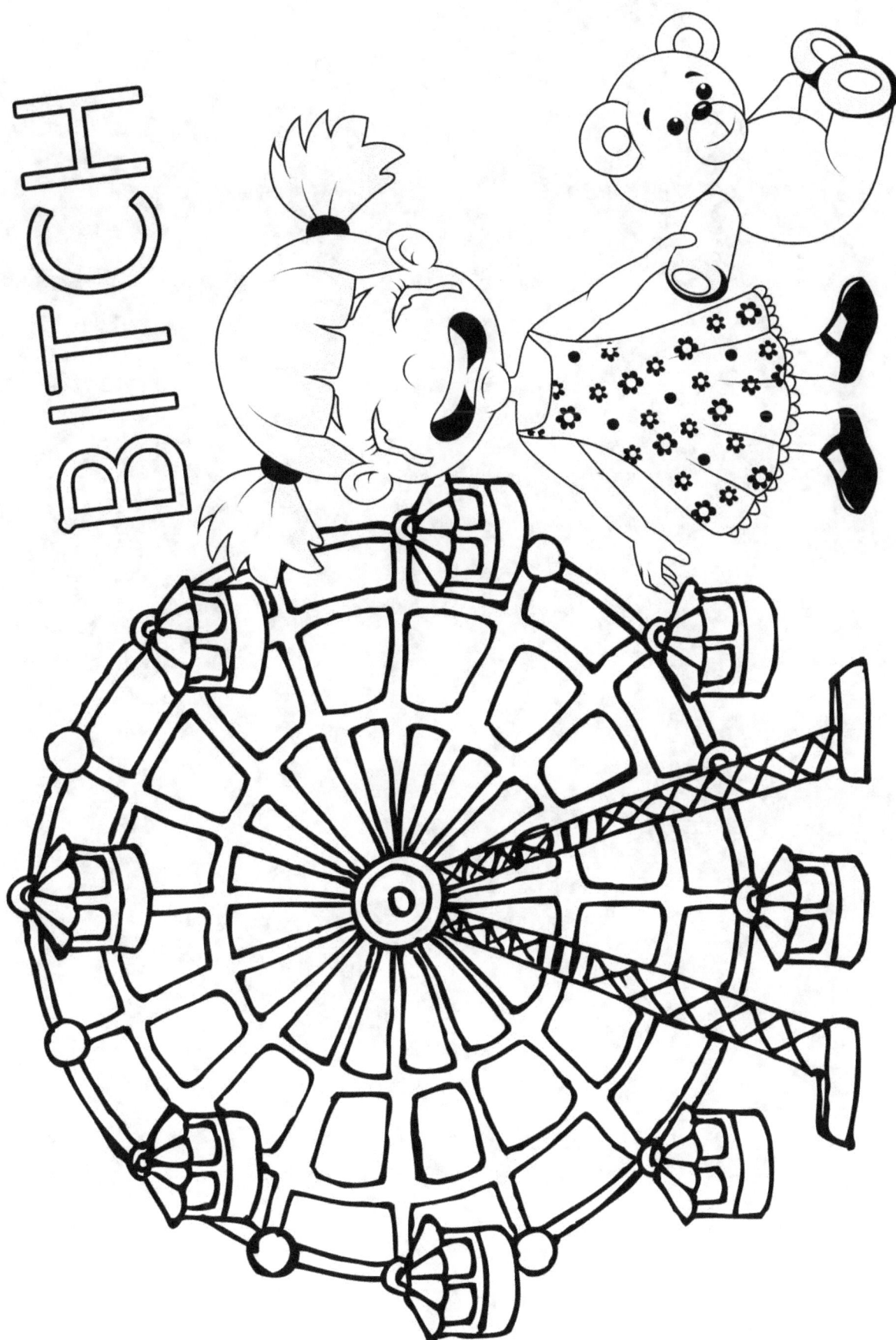

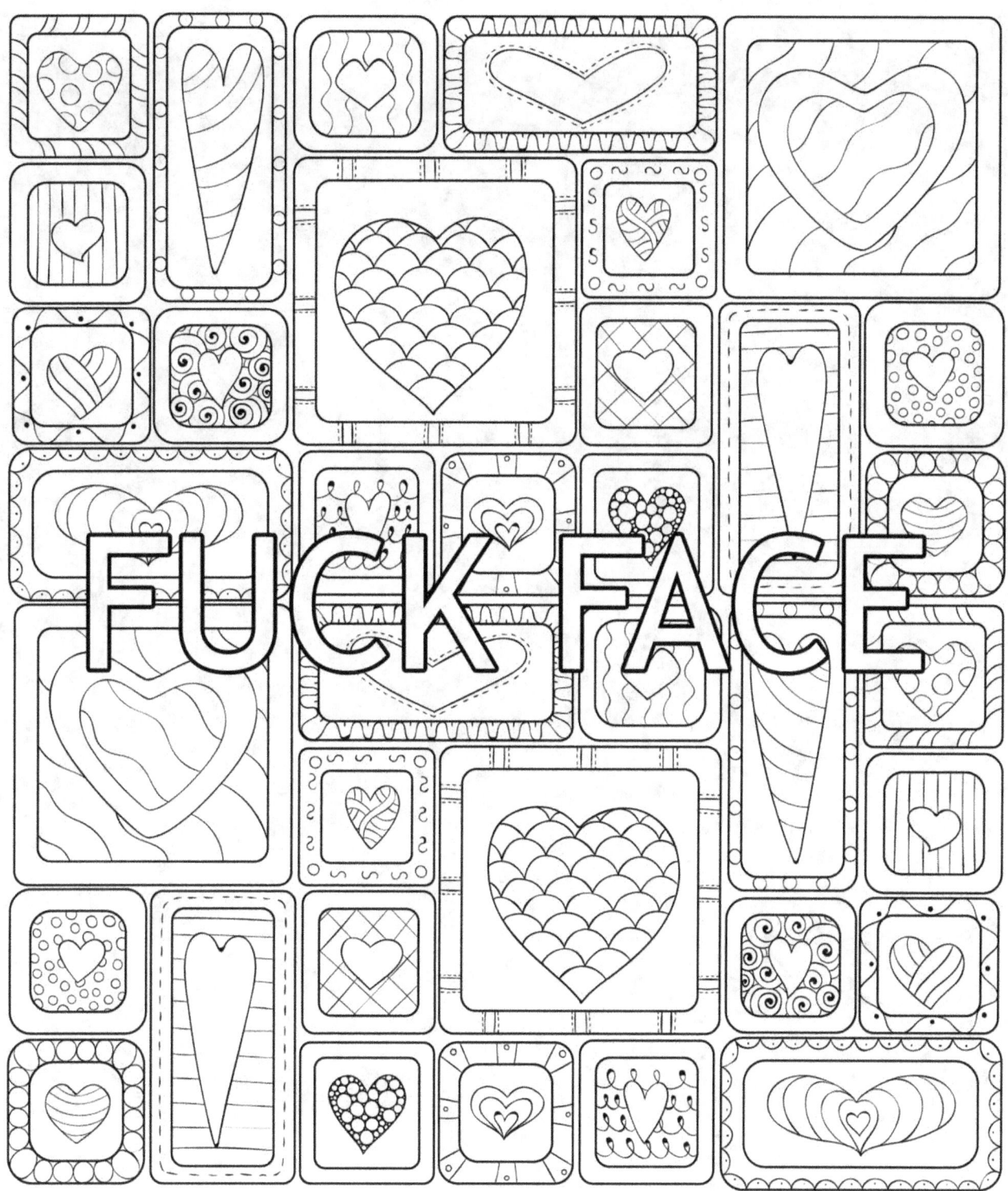

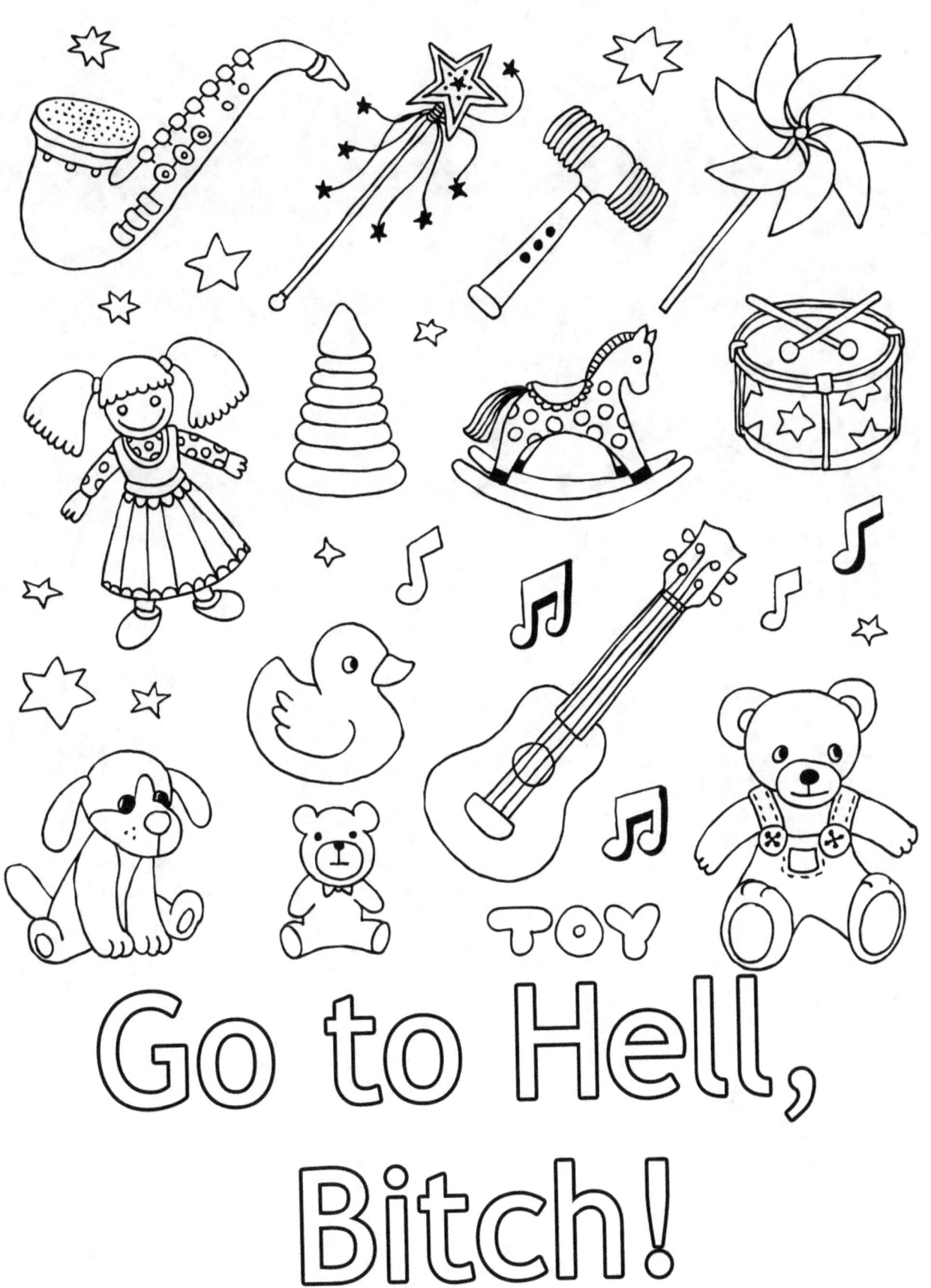

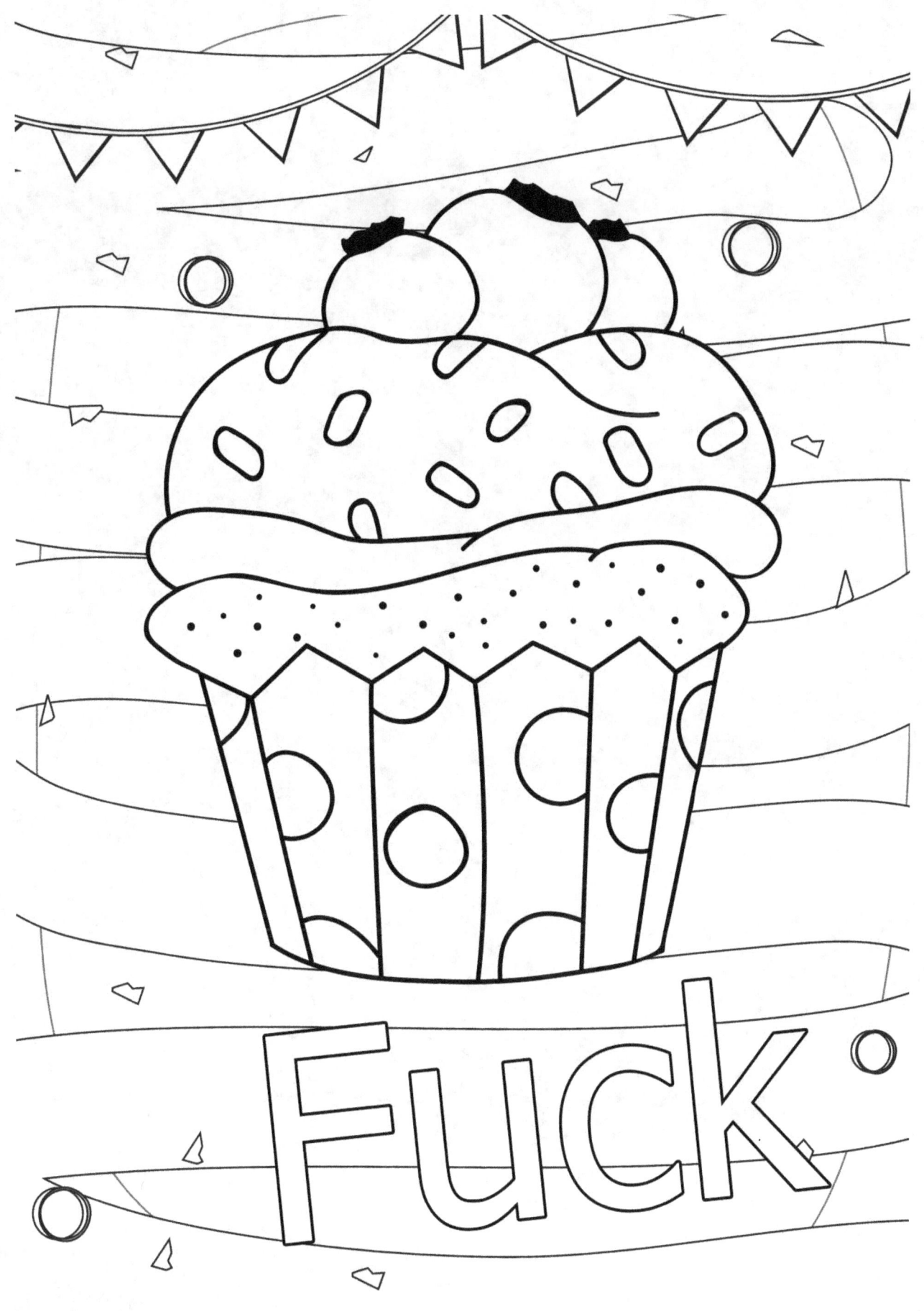

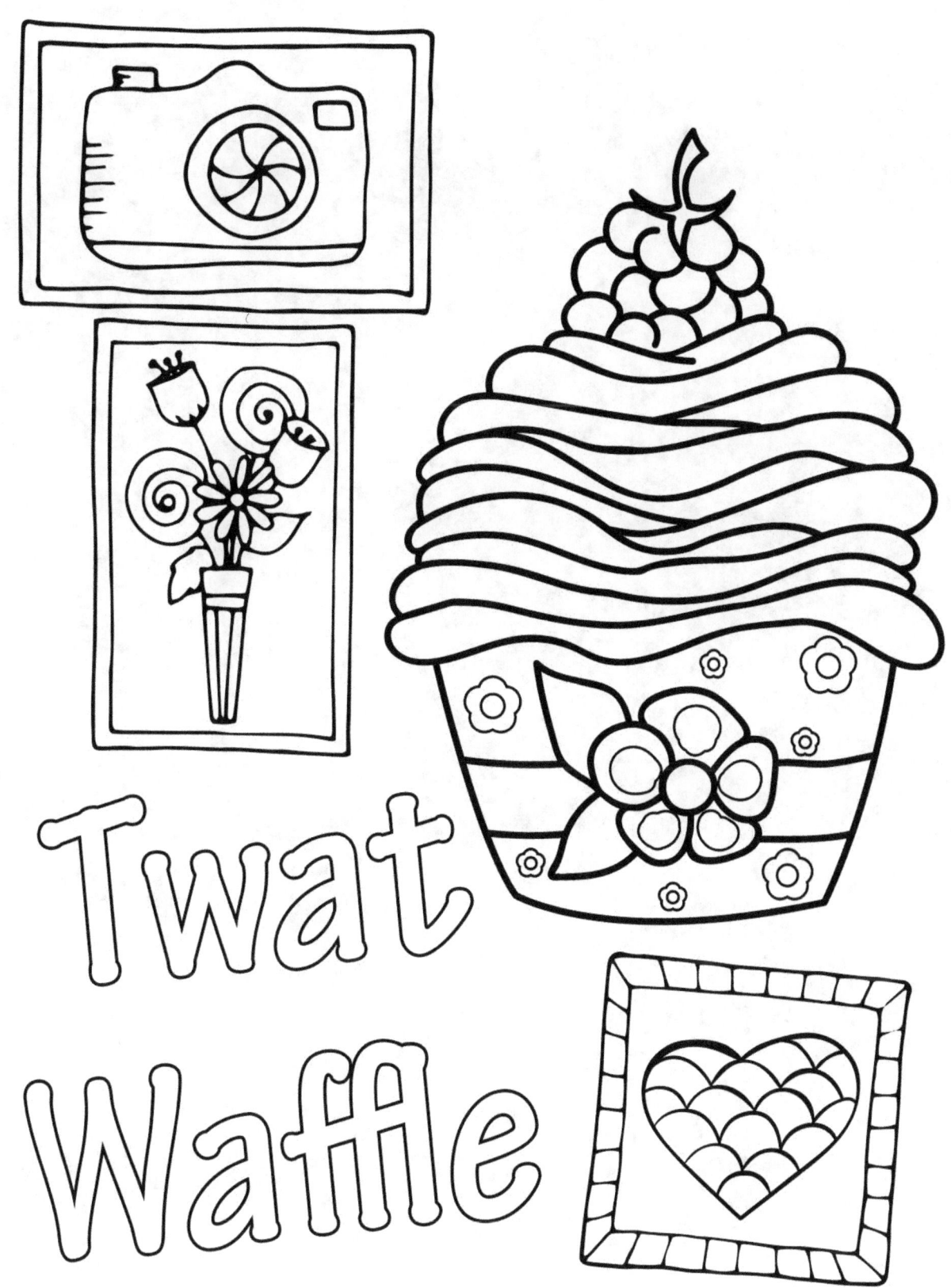

Twat Waffle

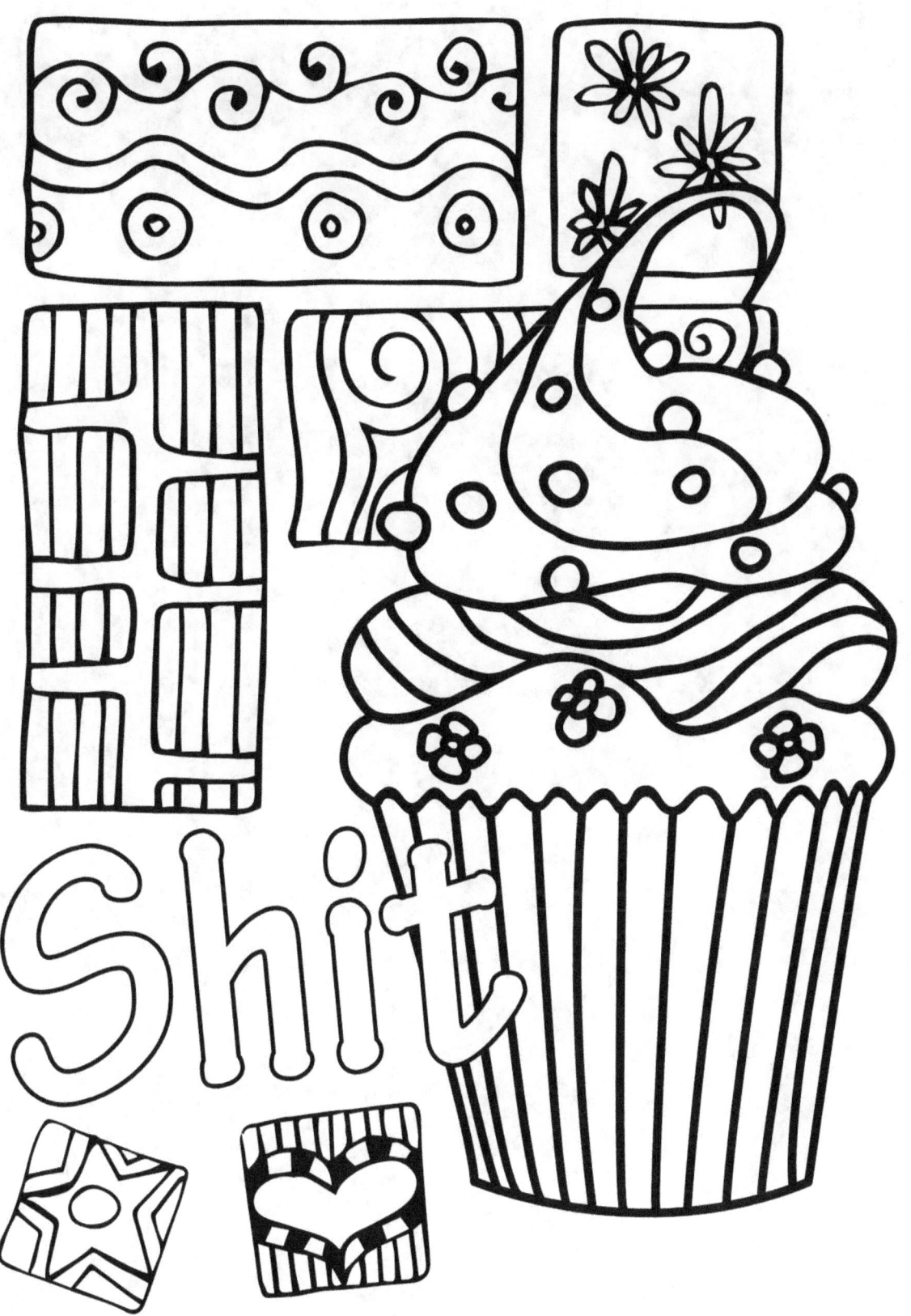

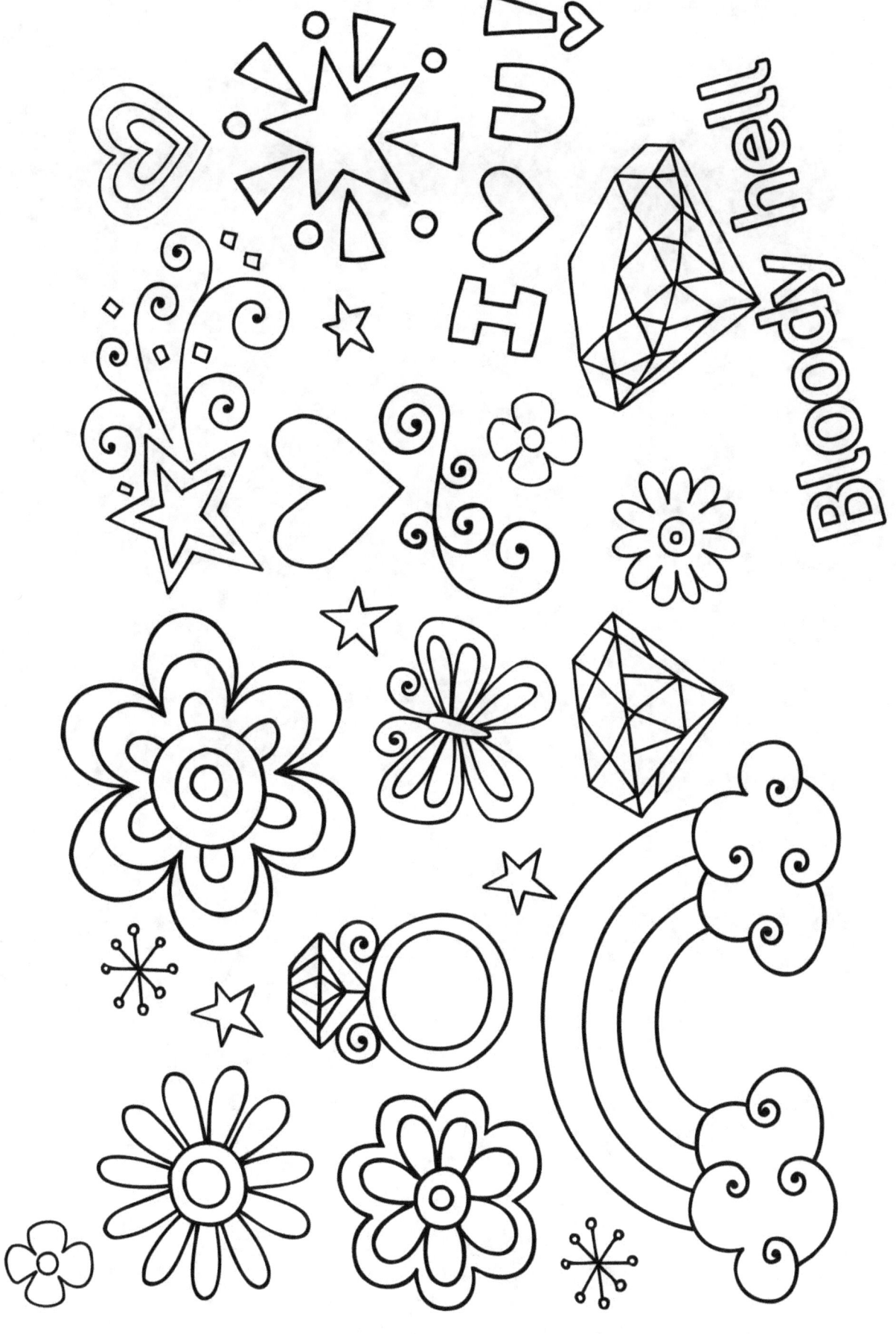

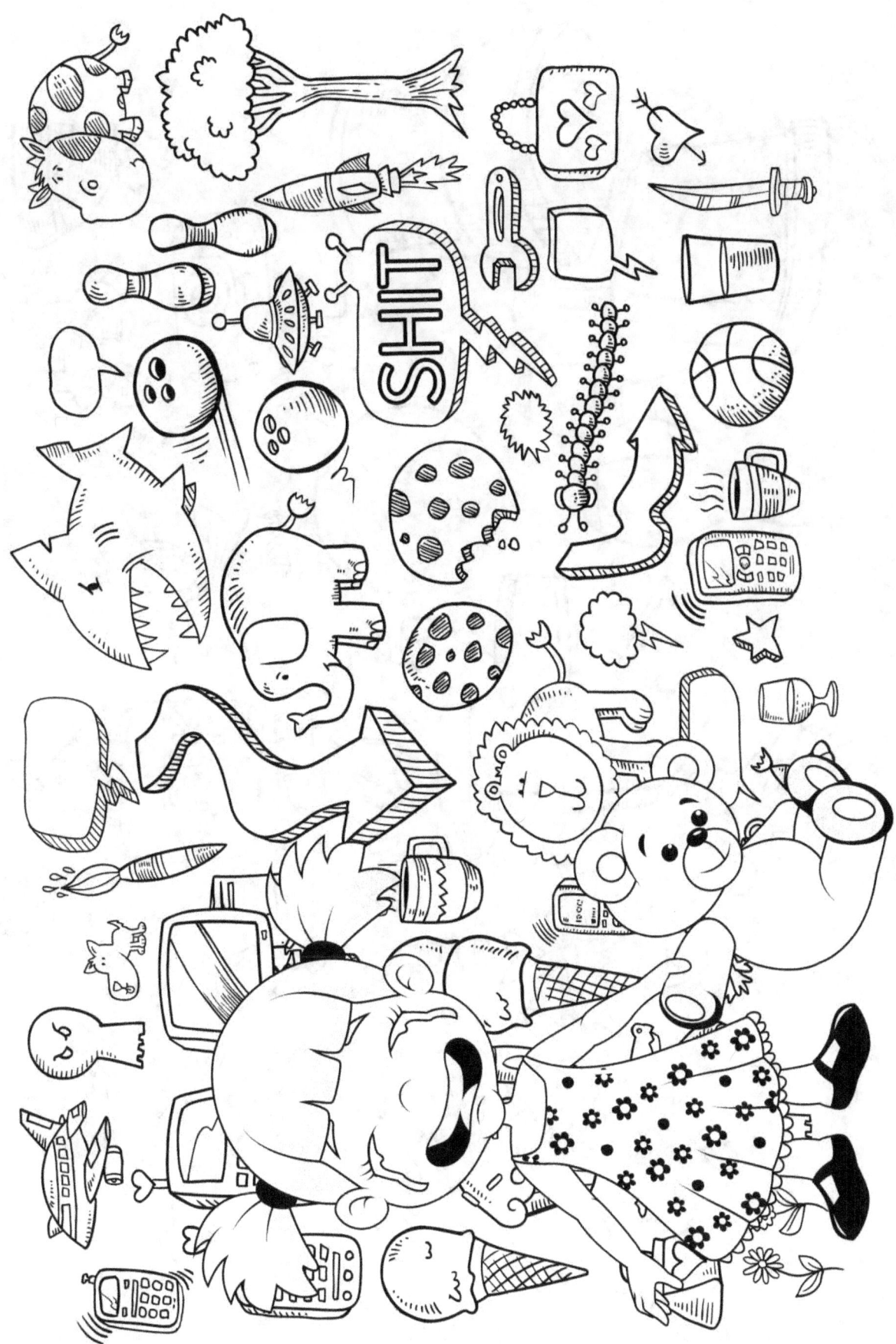

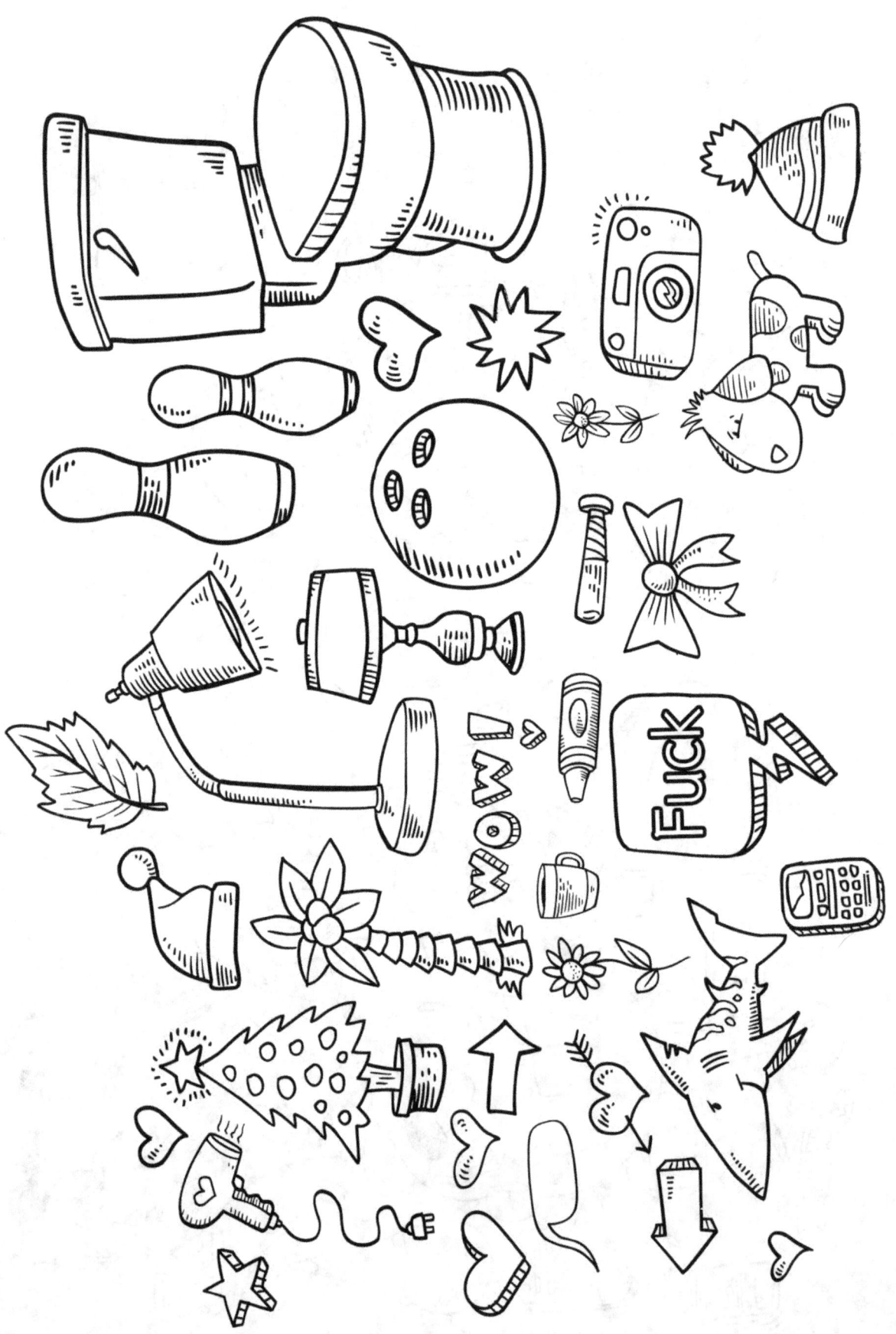

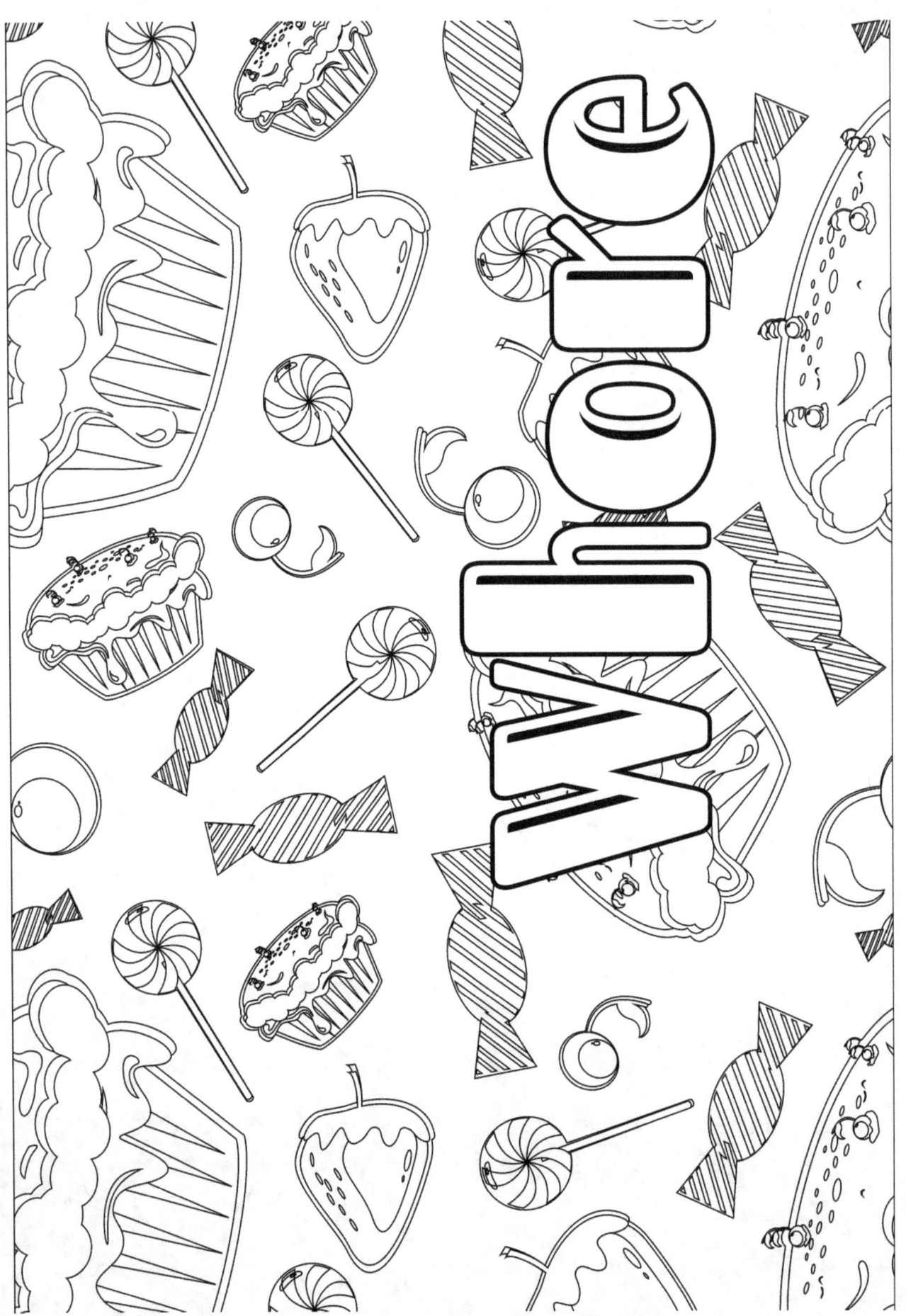

www.ingramcontent.com/pod-product-compliance
Lightning Source LLC
Chambersburg PA
CBHW081300180526
45170CB00007B/2505